C000121046

WHAT WOULD

THE

ROCK

DO?

POP PRESS

Pop Press, an imprint of Ebury Publishing,
20 Vauxhall Bridge Road,
London, SW1V 2SA

Pop Press is part of the Penguin Random House group of companies whose
addresses can be found at global.penguinrandomhouse.com

Penguin
Random House
UK

First published by Pop Press in 2021

www.penguin.co.uk

A CIP catalogue record for this book is available from the British Library

Design: Seagull Design
Illustrations: Ollie Mann

ISBN: 9781529108118

Typeset in 9.5/12 pt Futura Std
by Integra Software Services Pvt. Ltd, Pondicherry

Printed and bound in Great Britain by Clays Ltd, Elcograf S.p.A.

The authorised representative in the EEA is Penguin Random House Ireland,
Morrison Chambers, 32 Nassau Street, Dublin D02 YH68.

Penguin Random House is committed to a sustainable future for
our business, our readers and our planet. This book is made from
Forest Stewardship Council® certified paper.

CONTENTS

HOW TO
LIVE LIKE
THE ROCK

HOW TO LIVE LIKE THE ROCK

Everyone knows that The Rock is the nicest and hardest-working guy in Hollywood. He didn't get this reputation because of his natural charm, though, dear jabroni! It came from hard work and sheer grit with a *lot* of weight sessions over the years. You too can set your mind on anything you want to achieve and succeed, but it will take hard work and having your arse served to you a few times along the way. Come on, let's do this!

Early morning: Get up early (The Rock gets up at 4am – that might be a little too early for the rest of us mere mortals ...) and work out. Enjoy this quiet time because after this the rest of your day is going to be full on, as you're going to be so focused on achieving your goals, right?

Diet: Can you smell what The Rock is cooking? Remember, you are what you eat, so step away from the cookies and load up on protein instead. If you're having a cheat day, don't mess around and eat that giant plate of pancakes.

Mental health: The Rock knows first-hand what happens when you don't look after your own mental health. Working out will help, as will meditating and reminding yourself of your daily rules.

Winding down: Make sure you have some quiet time before you hit the sack. The Rock likes to spend up to two hours every evening reflecting on his day, going through his goals, having a cheeky glass of tequila and kicking back before another day of being the nicest man in Hollywood.

You're welcome.

SEVEN STEPS TO SUCCESS

If you want to be like The Rock, then you need to live by a set of rules that you should repeat to yourself every day in the mirror. Preferably shout 'Can you smell what [your name] is cooking?!' after reciting these rules.

1. Check your ego at the door

2. It pays to be nice

3. Always be the hardest worker in the room

4. You can succeed by using your own two hands

5. Failing spurs you on to succeed

6. Consistency is key

7. Always be yourself

FITNESS

'Lifting weights is why I don't need therapy today.'

'The men I idolised built their bodies and became somebody – like Sylvester Stallone and Arnold Schwarzenegger – and I thought, That can be me.'

*'It (training)
becomes my sense
of meditation.'*

'Women and pizza.'

**When asked what he eats
on a cheat day**

'We should never compare ourselves to others.'

*'Working out
anchors my day.'*

'For me, training is my meditation, my yoga, hiking, biking, therapy all rolled into one.'

'I work out, I hydrate, I drink tequila.'

'Working out is
my therapy, and
it's cheaper than
a shrink.'

'With a basic movement, with old-school movements, you can never go wrong. But the key is always form. Form is everything.'

MOTIVATION

'I like to use the hard times of the past to motivate me today.'

*'Leaving it all ...
means you give
every f–ing ounce
of effort you can.'*

'Blood, sweat and respect. The first two you give, the last one you earn.'

'I like making things that make people feel good.'

'1995. Seven bucks
in my pocket.
I knew two things:
I'm broke as hell
and one day
I won't be.'

'This place has something nowhere else does. You.'

'Don't worry about being the next me, be the first you.'

'I always feel like I want to take care of the audience first.'

'*Remember the
hard times.*'

'I've realised that the number one thing that keeps me motivated and positive is operating like my back's against the wall.'

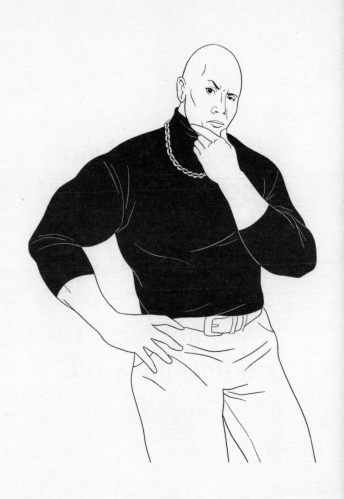

PHILOSOPHY

'It's nice to be important, but it's more important to be nice.'

'I need *to talk about
my issues and fears.
Not only am I okay
with it – I actually
enjoy it.*'

'You get so much
further with
optimism and
hope.'

'Respect is given
when it's earned, so
go out and earn it.'

'The most powerful thing that we can be is ourselves.'

'Depression doesn't discriminate.'

*'Life is much easier
when you're nice
and not full of shit.'*

'We've always got
to do our best to
pay attention when
other people are in
pain. We have to
help them through
it and remind them
they are not alone.'

'Being nice and kind is literally the easiest thing we can do.'

'I walk what I talk, daily, which I think is an important quality.'

FAME

'I was in the wrong game. And now I'm in the right one.'

'The ambition to grow developed the moment I stepped foot in Hollywood.'

'I wasn't going
to conform to
Hollywood;
Hollywood was
going to conform
to me.'

'I had no clue what I was doing, the only thing I knew that I was willing to do was to put in the work with my own two hands.'

'You align yourself smarter so you can achieve what you want to achieve. In my case that's a little thing I call world domination.'

'It's the easiest part of my job to be kind, take pictures and sign autographs.'

*'The greatest thing
I appreciate is
the fans.'*

'Things happen so quickly and I want you to know that I never take it for granted.'

'It took me about seven to eight years to realise that I'm done trying to conform to Hollywood.'

'The big stars didn't look like me and I didn't look like them. There wasn't a blueprint or a model. "Well, here's a former football player who once wrestled and he's this height and this weight. He's black and Samoan and he has tattoos ..."'

WRESTLING

'Can you smell
what The Rock is
cooking?'

'I'll always be known as The Rock!'

'Why don't you drink a big, tall glass of shut-up juice?'

'It doesn't matter!'

'I had been sulking on the sofa just watching trashy TV until that point. I decided there and then that, even if it wasn't in football, the world was still going to hear from me. That's pretty much where my wrestling career started.'

'Who in the blue hell are you?'

'By the time The Rock was born, I knew it would work out. Failure just wasn't an option.'

'Know your role
and shut your
mouth.'

'The Rock is going to go out there and do his thing. If you like it: great. If you don't like it: great too.'

'"You can't see me?" What are you playing? Peekaboo?'

FAMILY

'I will do honestly anything to bring a smile to my babies' faces.'

'I want someone who can trust that my big hands are going to take care of them.'

'I feel there's something powerful when a man reaches a point in his life when he can be completely vulnerable, completely honest, completely truthful.'

'My daughters taught me how to be more caring. More sensitive. More selfless.'

'Becoming a father
has inspired me
and motivated me
beyond words
that I can possibly
explain.'

'Guys don't mature until much, much later, so it's nice to be in my fourth level and have babies again.'

'The only thing that
I love more than
saving lives is my
daughter.'

'[I'm] surrounded by
estrogen. Bring on
the estrogen!'

'When I love you, I can really love you, whether it's my ex-wife or my girlfriend or my little girl or my friends, my guys, my buddies. Whatever it is, I value that relationship.'

'Ironically, when
you're not looking
for something,
the power of the
universe kind of
takes over.'

FILMS

'I was born of the sea. I eat fire coral and I piss salt water. I scratch my back with a whale's dick, and I loofah my chest with his ballsack.'

Baywatch

'Strengths: fearless, speed, smoldering intensity.'

Jumanji

'I'm trying to save the world, which, for the record, will be my fourth time, because I'm really good at it.'

Fast & Furious Presents: Hobbs & Shaw

'I may be a king,
but I'm a wrestler
first.'

The Scorpion King

'Ricky, here's my
first bit of financial
advice. Don't invest
in depreciating
assets. If it drives,
flies, floats or f–s,
lease it.'

Ballers

'When you use a
bird to write, it's
called tweeting.'

Moana

'You just earned
yourself a dance
with the devil,
boy. You're under
arrest!'

Furious 7

'I will beat your ass like a Cherokee drum!'

The Fate of the Furious

'Stay the fuck outta
my way.'

Fast Five

'Jesus Christ himself
has blessed me
with many gifts.
One of them is
knocking someone
the fuck out.'

Pain & Gain

SUCCESS

'Success isn't about greatness, it's about consistency.'

'Check your ego at the door. The ego can be the great success inhibitor. It can kill opportunities and it can kill success.'

'Arrogance and
the ego is one of
the key success
inhibitors.'

—

'Success doesn't happen without a foundation.'

'It (success) all comes down to your family and working hard to love and protect and do everything you can to make your family's and the ones you love lives better.'

'I'm a long way away from ever getting evicted again, but man, I think about that so much. That's where my "we've got to make sure this happens" and "let's go" type of energy comes from.'

*'I hope people
can look at my life
and see that hard
work and ambition
can take you a
long way.'*

'I am going to take a crack at this [his A-list career goals] and I have to be me, I have to be me.'

'My reputation
precedes me now.'

'Failing has become critical in my growth.'

WINNING

*'Do not go gentle –
because that rent is
always MF'n due.'*

'When you're good at something, you'll tell everyone. When you're great – they'll tell you.'

'It starts with what's in my gut, and what's in my gut is to entertain as many people as I can possibly entertain.'

'I'm gonna take care of you, the audience. You pay your hard-earned money – I don't need to bring my dark shit to you. Maybe a little – but if it's in there, we're gonna overcome it, and we're gonna overcome it together.'

*'You never want
to do anything
half-assed.'*

'You've got to be fucking tired of not being number one. And you've got to play fucking angry.'

'Be hungry, be humble and always make sure you are the hardest-working person in the room.'

'You need to believe that you are good enough and that you can accomplish what you set your mind to do.'

'It's fundamentals:
show up, outwork
everyone, and rely
on my own two
hands to get the
job done.'

'You want to be the hardest worker in the room but you also want to the smartest worker in the room.'

POLITICS

'I would get the minority vote as everyone just assumes that I'm whatever they are.'

Talking about running for President

'If I felt I could step up to the plate and become a tremendous leader and make a real difference and change, I would do it [run for President].'

'I'm not delusional at all and, you know what it is, I need that thing, what's it called? Oh yes, experience.'

'We'll have three days off for a weekend! No taxes!'

'*Surely the White House has a spot for my pick-up truck ...*'

'The Rock Obama
much like Barack
Obama, only
stronger and more
impulsive.'

*'The Rock Obama
is polite so I ask
"Please may I crush
your head?"'*

'While it is extremely flattering that a good amount of people feel that I should run for president, or make a decent president, or not suck at a being president, at the end of the day, I have a tremendous amount of respect for that position.'

'I love my country, I'm extremely patriotic and I also feel, especially now, leadership is so important, great leadership is so important, respected leadership is so important.'

'I believe in inclusion. Our country was built on that.'

ACKNOWLEDGEMENTS

p6 from *Muscle and Fitness*, 'Dwayne '"The Rock"' Johnson's 7 life lessons', p7 from Redbook, 'Dwayne Johnson Goes Soft on Us' (2012), p8 from *The Late Late Show* interview (2017), p9 from KISS FM UK interview, 'Dwayne Johnson talks WWE, Fighting Conor McGregor and New Movie Rampage' (2018), p10 from Kjersti Flaa interview, 'The Rock talks body insecurities (yes, he has them too)' (2017), p11 and 12 from Bodybuilding.com, 'Dwayne Johnson's Rock-Hard Hercules Workout And Diet Plan' (2020), p13 from *WSJ Magazine*, 'The Rock, From Strength to Strength' (2019), p14 from Bodybuilding.com, 'Train Like Dwayne "The Rock" Johnson!' (2020), p15 from *Muscle and Fitness*, 'Mythical Proportions: An Exclusive Interview with Dwayne "The Rock" Johnson', p18 from the *Daily Mail*, '"You never know": Dwayne '"The Rock"' Johnson says it's possible depression could strike again as he draws hundreds of fans at Hercules screening in Sydney' (2014), p19 from Dwayne Johnson's Instagram, p20 from 'The Rock's Ultimate Workout' (2017), p21 from Forbes, 'Why The Rock's Social Media Muscle Made Him Hollywood's Highest-Paid Actor' (2018), p22 from Dwayne Johnson's Twitter, p23 from *Fast & Furious Presents: Hobbs & Shaw* (2019), p24 from *Fighting with My Family*, p25 from *Independent*, 'Literally just 3 minutes with Dwayne "The Rock" Johnson, the biggest movie star on the planet' (2018), p26 from 'Teaching the Los Angeles Lakers How to Be World Champions: Dwayne Johnson's "Genius Talk" Part 1' (2018), p27 from *Entertainment Weekly*, 'Dwayne Johnson sleighs the holidays on *EW*'s new cover' (2017), p30 from Forbes, 'Why The Rock's Social Media Muscle Made Him Hollywood's Highest-Paid Actor' (2018), p31 from *Oprah's 2020 Vision: Your Life in Focus Tour* (2020), p32 from *The New York Times*, 'Dwayne Johnson, Star of '"San Andreas,"' Is Solid. Solid as a …' (2015), p33 from *Judith Regan Tonight* (1999), p34 from Generation Award at MTV Movie and TV Awards (2019), p35 from *Lorraine* interview (2018), p36 from Forbes, 'How Dwayne "The Rock" Johnson Became The World's Biggest Star' (2018), p37 from *Daily Express*, 'Dwayne "The Rock" Johnson: My secret battle with depression' (2018), p38 from Off Script interview with Jamie Foxx (2018), p39 from Reuters, '"The Rock"' talks a future in politics, including potential White House run' (2016), p42 from *Sports Illustrated*, 'How football helped transform Dwayne Johnson into Hollywood's biggest star' (2016), p43 from Variety, 'Dwayne Johnson on His Rock-Solid Empire and Walk of Fame Honor' (2017), p44 from Generation Award at MTV Movie and TV Awards (2019), p45 from *The Jimmy Kimmel Show* interview (2017), p46 from People, 'Dwayne Johnson: Soft on the Inside' (2019), p47 from Live with Kelly and Ryan interview (2019), p48 from The Rock Reacts to His First WWE Match: 20 Years of The Rock (2016), p49 from June Lift: The Rock Shows Us How to Hip Thrust (2017), p50 from *TIME*, 'Dwayne Johnson Opens Up About His Childhood, Trying To Fit Into Hollywood & More' (2019), p51 from *Esquire*, 'The Rock Is Dead. Long Live Dwayne Johnson, American Treasure' (2015), p54, 55, p54, 56, 57, 59, 61, and 63 from WWE p55 from *This Morning* interview (12 April 2018), p58 and p60 from *Esquire*, 'The Esquire interview: Dwayne "The Rock" Johnson' (2018), p62 from *Off the Record* (1999), p66 from Fatherly, 'The Rock on His Daughters, Divorce, and Being the Nicest Guy in Hollywood' (2019), p67 and p68 from *Essence* 'Solid as a Rock' (2013), p69 from *Oprah's 2020 Vision: Your Life in Focus Tour* (2020), p70 from *Good Morning America* interview (2016), p71 from *Rolling Stone*, 'Dwayne Johnson: The Pain and the Passion That Fuel the Rock' (2018), p72 from *The Fate of the Furious* (2017), p73 from *The Jimmy Kimmel Show* interview (2017), p74 from CNN Official Interview: Dwayne Johnson on his manager/ex-wife (2011), p75 *WSJ Magazine*, 'The Rock, From Strength to Strength' (2019), p78 from *Baywatch* (2017), p79 from *Jumanji* (2017), p80 from *Fast & Furious Presents: Hobbs & Shaw* (2019), p81 from *The Scorpion King* (2002), p82 from *Ballers*, p83 from *Moana* (2016), p84 from *Furious 7* (2015), p85 *The Fate of the Furious* (2017), p86 from *Fast Five* (2011), p87 from *Pain & Gain* (2013), p90 from Dwayne Johnson's Twitter, p91 from *GQ*, 'Dwayne Johnson's 5 rules for living' (2016), p92 from *Elle*, 'The Rock is Great at Losing his Virginity and Checking His Ego' (2017), p93 and p94 from Hollywood Walk of Fame speech (2017), p95 from *Esquire*, 'The Rock Is Dead. Long Live Dwayne Johnson, American Treasure' (2015), p96 from *Squaremile*, 'Dwayne Johnson Interview | The Rock on Baywatch, The Fate of the Furious and being the world's highest-paid actor' (2017), p97 from *The New York Times* 'Dwayne Johnson, Star of "San Andreas,"' Is Solid. Solid as a …' (2015), p98 from *Fortune*, 'The Rock's Best Advice for Success' (2014), p99 from WWE 'How The Rock Found Success in Failure' interview (2012), p102 from Dwayne Johnson's Facebook, p103 from Dwayne Johnson's Facebook, p104 from Variety, 'Dwayne Johnson on His Rock-Solid Empire and Walk of Fame Honor' (2017), p105 from *Rolling Stone* 'Dwayne Johnson: The Pain and the Passion That Fuel the Rock' (2018), p106 from Goalcast, 'Dwayne "The Rock" Johnson: Find Your Anchor' (2017), p107 from Los Angeles Lakers Genius Talk (2018), p108 from SilverKris, 'Dwayne Johnson: "Make sure you're the hardest-working person in the room"' (2018), p109 from Square Mile, 'Dwayne Johnson Interview' (2017), p110 from Fortune, 'The Rock's Best Advice for Success' (2014), p111 from People TV (2016), p114 from *Saturday Night Live*, 'Dwayne Johnson Five-Timers Monologue' (2017), p115 from ABC News, 'The Rock Reveals Political Aspirations' (2016), p116 from *The Late Show with Stephen Colbert* interview (2018), p117 from *GQ*, 'Dwayne Johnson for President!' (2017), p118 from Dwayne Johnson's Twitter, p119 from *Saturday Night Live*, 'The Rock Obama: GOP Senators' (2013), p120 from *Saturday Night Live*, 'The Rock Obama Cold Open' (2015), p121 from Indiewire, 'Dwayne Johnson: 'I'm Not Ruling Out' a Presidential Run After 2020' (2019), p122 from Reuters, 'The Rock' talks a future in politics, including potential White House run' (2016), and p123 from *GQ*, 'Dwayne Johnson for President' (2017).